GREAT MOMENTS IN AMERICAN HISTORY

Democracy's Signature

Benjamin Franklin and the Declaration of Independence

Danny Fingeroth

ROSEN CENTRAL
PRIMARY SOURCE™

THE ROSEN PUBLISHING GROUP, INC., NEW YORK

Published in 2004 by The Rosen Publishing Group, Inc.
29 East 21st Street, New York, NY 10010

Editor: Eric Fein
Book Design: Michelle Innes
Photo researcher: Rebecca Anguin-Cohen
Series photo researcher: Jeff Wendt

Photo Credits: Cover (left), title page, p. 22, Architect of the Capitol, cover (right)
illustration © Debra Wainwright/The Rosen Publishing Group; p. 6 New York Historical
Society/ The Bridgeman Art Library; pp. 10, 31 © North Wind Pictures Archive; pp. 14, 29
© Hulton/Archive/Getty Images; p. 18 From the Collection of Gilcrease Museum, Tulsa, OK;
p. 30 courtesy of the Westchester County Historical Society; p. 32 Library of Congress
Manuscript Division, George Washington Papers

First Edition

Library of Congress Cataloging-in-Publication Data

Fingeroth, Danny
    Democracy's signature : Benjamin Franklin and the Declaration of Independence/
    Danny Fingeroth.
        p.   cm. — (Great moments in American history)
    Summary: Benjamin Franklin, who had worked for a peaceful solution to the problems
    of the colonies, signs the document that declares the independence of the colonies.
    ISBN 0-8239-4332-1 (lib. bdg.)
    1. Franklin, Benjamin, 1706-1790—Juvenile literature 2. United States. Declaration of
    Independence— Signers—Biography—Juvenile literature 3. United States—Politics
    and government—1775-1783—Juvenile literature   [1. Franklin, Benjamin, 1706-
    1790 2. Statesmen   3. United States. Declaration of Independence—Signers   4.
    United States—Politics and government—1775-1783] I. Title   II. Series

    973.3'092—dc21
    [B]
                                                                    2003-004353

Manufactured in the United States of America

CONTENTS

❦

The American Revolutionary War was fought between England and its American colonies. The war lasted from 1775 to 1783. One of the main reasons for the war was that the colonists did not want to pay the high taxes that England demanded. Also, the colonists were angry because they did not have any representation in the British government.

From 1754 to 1763, England and France fought a war in America and Canada. The war cost England a lot of money. England's King George III tried to raise money by taxing the American colonists. Taxes were placed on many goods, such as tea and paper, that the colonists needed. The colonists had fought for England in the war. They felt that they were being unfairly taxed by the king.

The colonists grew angry with England. Sometimes fighting broke out between the British soldiers in America and the colonists. On April 19, 1775, a big battle between British soldiers and colonists took place in the towns of Lexington and Concord, Massachusetts. The Revolutionary War had begun.

Benjamin Franklin had been trying to find a peaceful solution to the problem before the war began. Franklin was from the colony of Pennsylvania. He was a successful printer and inventor. Franklin was also active in politics and was respected by his fellow colonists. In 1764, Franklin went to England to try to work out a settlement between the British and the American colonists. However, as time went on, he could see that there was little hope for a peaceful settlement.

Franklin returned to America from England in 1775. He found his beloved colonies at war with England, and himself fighting with his own family as well. . . .

Benjamin Franklin was born on January 17, 1706, in Boston, Massachusetts. At the age of twelve, he went to work in a print shop. In 1728, Franklin started his own print shop in Philadelphia, Pennsylvania.

Chapter One

A FAMILY DIVIDED

"You're wrong, Father. The colonies belong to England," said William Franklin, the governor of New Jersey. William was the son of Benjamin Franklin.

Ben Franklin shook his head sadly. "My son, you do not fully understand the situation," he said. It was August 1775. The troubles between the American colonists and England were getting worse.

"I understand that many colonists are being ungrateful to King George. How dare they refuse to pay taxes?" said William. "And how dare they use force against England's troops here in the colonies?"

Franklin looked around the large study in his son's New Jersey home. The room was filled with very expensive furniture. "I think you have become too comfortable. You see only what you want.

I spent over ten years in England trying to reach a settlement that would be fair to England and the colonies. For my efforts, I was made fun of and accused of treason by those you think so highly of. Until then, I thought there could be a peaceful solution to the problem. Now, I know better. England will not be satisfied until it has grounded the colonists down under its heel."

"You have a way with words, Father. Still, I am unmoved by your arguments. The other loyalists and I will support the king. We will do everything to put an end to this revolution. And you should not forget that you have ignored your family because of your work for the revolutionaries' cause. Your own wife, Deborah, died without you at her side."

Franklin slowly got to his feet. He suffered from gout, which caused pain in his legs. "My son," he said, "your words hurt me. I had hoped we could work together for the common good of the colonies. I was wrong."

"Perhaps you were," said William. His harsh tone softened a bit as he watched Franklin walk out of the room. For the first time he noticed how frail and old his father looked. Despite the fact that Franklin would soon turn seventy, William always thought of his father as a strong man.

In the hallway, near the front door, Franklin was greeted by his grandson, William Temple Franklin. William Temple had spent some time with his grandfather in England. He had worked as Franklin's secretary.

"Grandfather, I heard shouting. Were you arguing with Father?"

Franklin put a hand on the teenager's shoulder. "Your father and I disagree strongly over the fate of our people. But do not trouble yourself. I will not cut myself off from you."

Without another word, Franklin left the house. William Temple fought back tears as he closed the door. "Good-bye, Grandfather," he said in a voice no louder than a whisper.

Thomas Jefferson (left) brought his first draft of the Declaration of Independence to the home of Ben Franklin (right). Franklin made suggestions that helped Jefferson write the Declaration of Independence.

Chapter Two

THE COMMITTEE OF FIVE

In June 1776, Thomas Jefferson visited Ben Franklin at his home in Philadelphia, Pennsylvania. Jefferson represented the colonists of Virginia. He was in Philadelphia for meetings that the Continental Congress was holding. In 1774, the Continental Congress was formed by the colonists to deal with their problems with England.

"Mr. Franklin, it's good to see you, sir," said Jefferson, shaking Franklin's hand.

"Ah, Thomas, it's nice of you to visit. But what brings you to my home? Doesn't Congress have a full schedule to keep?" said Franklin.

Jefferson smiled. "You're quite right, sir. This is more than a friendly visit. Events are starting to come together very quickly. As I'm sure you have

heard, Richard Henry Lee of Virginia has put forth a resolution for colonial independence. However, Congress has postponed a vote on it until July. In the meantime, it has been decided that a document is needed to explain our actions to our people and the world."

"A good idea," said Franklin.

"A group, the Committee of Five, has been picked to write this document."

Franklin smiled broadly. "Don't tell me, I've been chosen as one of the five."

"Yes, sir," Jefferson said, nodding his head.

"And who else is joining me on this project?" Franklin asked.

"Myself, John Adams, Roger Sherman, and Robert Livingston," answered Jefferson.

"All good men. So what is expected of me?"

"I was hoping that you would write the first draft of the document."

Franklin laughed. "My dear Thomas, look at me. I am seventy years old and I am sick. I haven't the strength to write such an important

document. However, you are energetic and smart. You would be the perfect writer for this project."

"Me?" said a shocked Jefferson.

"You *do* have a way with words. I would be happy to read what you write and to offer my humble advice," Franklin said.

With Franklin's support, Jefferson went off to write the document. He spent many days writing it. When he was finished, he brought the document to Franklin. Franklin read it with great interest. "This is a wonderful piece of writing, Thomas. I have only a few points that you might want to consider.

"For instance, where you write 'We hold these truths to be sacred and undeniable,' I would have it read, 'We hold these truths to be self-evident.'" As Franklin spoke, Jefferson made notes. "I must tell you, Thomas, I'm a bit jealous of you. The document is well done. I wish I had written it."

"There is no greater compliment than that, sir," said Jefferson. "I just hope the rest of Congress feels the same as you."

s laws the most wholesome and ne

forbidden his governors to pass laws of immediate & pressing im

unless suspended in their operation till his assent should be obta

and when so suspended, he has *utterly* neglected utterly to attend to them.

he has refused to pass other laws for the accomodation of large districts of people

unless those people would relinquish the right of representation *in the legislature*, a right

inestimable to them, & formidable to tyrants only:

as dissolved Representative houses repeatedly & continually

manly firmness his invasions on the rights of the people:

~~dissolved~~, he has refused for a long ~~space of time~~ *time after such dissolutions* to cause others to be elected,

~~whereby the~~ legislative powers, incapable of annihilation, have ~~returned~~ to

the people at large for their exercise, the state remaining in the mean time

exposed to all the dangers of invasion from without, & convulsions within:

he has endeavored to prevent the population of these states; for that purpose

obstructing the laws for naturalization of foreigners; refusing to pass others

to encourage their migrations hither; & raising the conditions of new ap-

-propriations of lands:

he has suffered the administration of justice totally to cease in some of these

states refusing his assent to laws for establishing judiciary powers:

he has made [our] judges dependant on his will alone, for the tenure of their offices,

the + *& payment*
and amount of their salaries:

he has erected a multitude of new offices [by a self-assumed power,] & sent hi:

-ther swarms of officers to harrass our people & eat out their substance:

he has kept among us in times of peace, standing armies [& ships of war *without the consent of our*]

he has affected to render the military independent of & superior to the civil power:

he has combined with others to subject us to a jurisdiction foreign to

This is part of Thomas Jefferson's first draft of the Declaration of Independence. Jefferson made notes and changes on this document before he wrote the next draft.

Chapter Three

THE DEBATE BEGINS

*J*efferson spent the next several days getting the suggestions of the other members of the Committee of Five. He took their suggestions and put them into the next draft of the document he wrote.

In the meantime, Franklin's health was getting better. He enjoyed his home, which he shared with his daughter Sally, her husband Richard Bache, and their son Bennie. Yet he missed his son William. It had been almost a year since they had spoken.

The hurt was deepened when Franklin received a letter from William Temple. The letter read:
Dear Grandfather,

Things have taken a turn for the worse here. Father has been placed under house arrest by the New Jersey

Assembly. I am frightened. What will happen to him? What will happen to me?
Your Grandson, William Temple Franklin

Franklin quickly wrote back to his grandson:

Dear William,
I know things look uncertain. But do not lose hope. Though I am powerless to help your father, I will make sure you are taken care of.
Your Loving Grandfather

The members of Congress gathered on July 1. They settled into their seats in the Pennsylvania State House on Chestnut Street in Philadelphia. Once settled, they immediately began discussing Lee's resolution, which would declare the colonies free of British rule. Some members of Congress did not want to break away from England. They still believed that there was a chance to work things out with England.

All the while, Franklin sat quietly next to Thomas Jefferson, watching the arguments. In

the afternoon, the sunny sky clouded over and a thunderstorm drenched Philadelphia. Franklin looked out the window at the dark, gray sky and the flashes of lightning. He shifted in his chair. He was getting restless. He was losing patience with those who thought things could be worked out with England. He had once thought the same thing. He had spent over ten years of his life in England trying to find a peaceful solution to the troubles between England and its American colonies. But the king and England's government were not interested in the well-being of the colonists.

The next day, July 2, the members of Congress finally came to an agreement. The resolution was passed. A new chapter in America's history had just been written. Now, attention was turned to the one document that would state the colonists cause clearly to the world—the Declaration of Independence.

Benjamin's son, William Franklin, was made governor of New Jersey in 1762. After William refused to take the colonies' side against England, he and his father were never again friendly toward each other.

Chapter Four

DISCUSSING THE DECLARATION

*J*uly 3 was a bright, sunny day. Franklin was up early and at his usual seat in the meeting room. Once again, Thomas Jefferson sat by his side. Before the meeting began, other matters needed to be taken care of. This included the reading of letters sent by the colonies' military leaders. Some letters reported the happenings in the colonies. Other letters contained requests for men and supplies. Among the letters were papers from New Jersey's government. One of these papers was a copy of a letter from General George Washington. Washington's letter was directed at one of his officers. In the letter, Washington scolded the officer for not doing his job. The officer had been given the task of moving William

Franklin from New Jersey to a prison in Litchfield, Connecticut.

The letter was read out loud. All the members of Congress heard it. Some looked at Franklin. They felt bad for him. Others did not look at him because they did not want to embarrass him by staring. For his part, Franklin sat silent and calm. *William, I am sorry that this has happened,* he thought to himself. *This is a sad event. As I sit here helping to unite the colonies into one country—one family—my own family has fallen apart.*

Shortly, the members of Congress settled down to the business of rewriting Jefferson's document. The document was read out loud. After each section was read, it was discussed. The changes were noted and the next part was read.

Franklin looked over at Jefferson. Jefferson looked quite upset. The members were arguing about cutting a passage out of the document.

Jefferson wanted it to stay in. However, he knew he had no control over the editing of the document. Still, it upset him greatly to see his work changed. Jefferson noticed Franklin watching him. "They are undoing all my hard work, Mr. Franklin," he stated quietly.

"Don't worry, Thomas," said Franklin. "You have served your countrymen well. Being rewritten is the price you pay for writing anything that will be reviewed by a group of people with the power to make changes."

Franklin then told Jefferson a funny story to brighten his mood. It did. At the end of the day, the members of Congress had not finished rewriting the document. It was decided that the work would continue the next day.

This painting was made around 1817 by John Trumbull. It shows all the members of the Continental Congress about to sign the final draft of the Declaration of Independence.

Chapter Five

Signing the Declaration of Independence

The next day, July 4, the members of the Continental Congress turned their attention to Jefferson's document. Again, they began going through the document, studying every sentence and every word. At times there was much shouting as everyone tried to make his point. The pressure was on them: A decision needed to be made—and soon. More British troops were arriving in the colonies. On June 28, British warships had attacked Charleston, South Carolina. The next day, more British warships were seen off the coast of New York.

The disagreements over how the document should read continued. Jefferson, looking worried, turned to Franklin. "Why can they not agree?"

"Dear Thomas, when you assemble a large number of people to benefit from their intelligence and experience, you will also get their personal interests and their flaws, too," Franklin replied.

Finally, in the afternoon, Congress agreed on the exact wording of the document. The Declaration of Independence was approved. John Hancock, the president of Congress, ordered copies of the document to be made. An engrossed copy was also ordered. The engrossed copy would be written in large, clear handwriting on parchment paper. Word of the declaration spread throughout all thirteen colonies. Newspapers printed the declaration. People gathered to hear it read aloud.

On August 2, 1776, the engrossed copy of the Declaration of Independence was ready to be signed by the members of Congress. Before he signed the Declaration of Independence, Ben Franklin read it over carefully. John Hancock was amused by Franklin's actions. He said to

Franklin, "Come, come, sir. We must be as one. We must all hang together."

Everyone laughed. Franklin nodded in agreement and said as he signed, "Indeed we must all hang together. Otherwise we shall most assuredly hang separately."

All my years of hard work have finally paid off, Franklin thought to himself. *The colonies are now well on their way to independence.* Then, his smile faded a bit as he thought of the cost of his hard work. His wife died while he was in England. Then, he lost his son over their disagreement.

After the signing, Congress continued to ask Franklin for his help. He was honored. He wrote to a friend: "I have only a few years to live, and I am resolved to devote them to the work that my fellow citizens deem proper of me."

Franklin was soon sent to France to get its help in fighting the British. France was a wonderful country. It was a place of fine art and writing. Many important people lived there.

It would be a good learning opportunity for his grandsons, who would make the trip with him.

On October 26, 1776, Franklin waited on the dock to board the ship that would take him to France. Then, he saw his grandson, William Temple. "Grandfather!" shouted William, arms outstretched as he ran toward Franklin.

"Easy, William, I'm not as sturdy as I used to be," said Franklin, hugging his grandson.

Together, with Franklin's younger grandson, Bennie, they boarded a ship named *Reprisal*. The three of them stood on the deck watching the land pass as they sailed down the Delaware River.

"Isn't this exciting, Grandfather?" said Bennie.

Franklin put an arm around each grandson's shoulders. "Yes," he said. "We shall accomplish many great things in France."

The future looks bright, Franklin thought. *But not just for the country. It's brighter for me, too. My family is together again.*

GLOSSARY

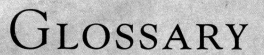

assembly (uh-SEM-blee) a meeting of many people

colonies (KOL-uh-neez) territories that have been
settled by people from another country and is
controlled by that country

**Declaration of Independence (dek-luh-RAY-shuhn
UHV in-di-PEN-duhnss)** a document declaring
the freedom of the thirteen American colonies
from British rule

engrossed (en-GROHSD) to have been copied or
written in large letters

gout (GOWT) a painful illness that affects the joints

parchment (PARCH-muhnt) heavy, paperlike material
made from the skin of sheep or goats and used for
writing on

resolution (rez-uh-LOO-shuhn) a formal expression of
opinion, will, or intent voted on by an official group

revolution (rev-uh-LOO-shun) a violent uprising by
the people of a country that changes its system of
government

Primary Sources

How can we learn about events that happened hundreds of years ago? Studying sources such as old letters, paintings, diaries, maps, and newspapers is one way. These sources help us understand the history-making people and events of long ago. For example, the painting on page 30 shows the Declaration of Independence being read to a crowd of people in New York in 1776. By analyzing the painting, we can identify the kind of clothing that the colonists wore. We can compare and contrast how people dressed in the 1770s to how they dress today.

The painting also helps us to construct a story about what it might have been like to be at the reading of the Declaration of Independence on that day. Sources such as this painting bring the past to life and help us answer questions about important events.

The group chosen to write the Declaration of Independence was called the Committee of Five. The committee was made up of Ben Franklin, Thomas Jefferson, John Adams, Robert Livingston, and Roger Sherman.

After the Declaration of Independence was signed, copies were made and sent out to all the colonies. This picture shows the Declaration of Independence being read to people in White Plains, New York, on July 11, 1776.

Franklin took both of his grandsons, William Temple and Bennie Bache, when he went to France in 1776.

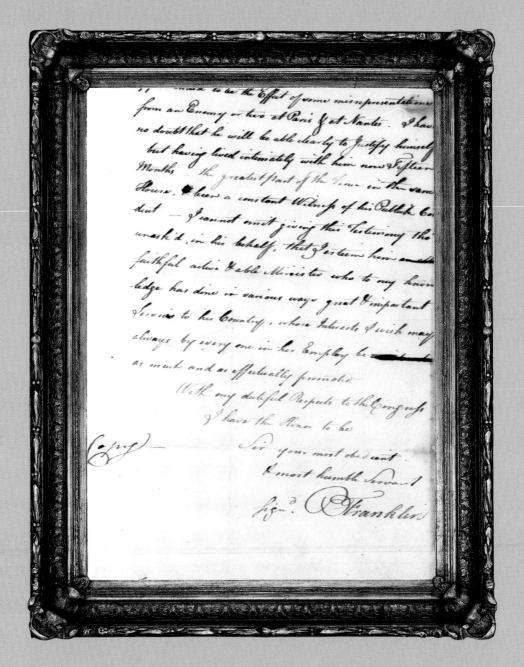

Franklin sent many reports back to the colonies about his work in France. This report was written to the Continental Congress on March 31, 1778. It tells Congress about the good work done by Silas Deane who went to France with Franklin.